The Peregrine's Journey

A STORY OF MIGRATION

MADELEINE DUNPHY   Illustrated by KRISTIN KEST

Web of Life

CHILDREN'S BOOKS

For Shannon, Siobhan, Joana and Sofia.
　　　　　—MD

To my beloved S^2 with gratitude.
　　　　　—K^2

For more information about our books, and the authors and artists who create
them, visit us online at www.weboflifebooks.com, or write to:
Web of Life Children's Books · P.O. Box 2726 · Berkeley, California 94702

Published in the United States in 2008 by Web of Life Children's Books.
Second printing 2014. Third printing 2015. Fourth printing 2017. Fifth printing 2018.
Sixth printing 2019. Seventh printing 2019. Eighth printing 2020.

Distributed by Publishers Group West, an Ingram Brand

Printed in Malaysia.

Library of Congress Control Number: 2007930013

ISBN 0-9777539-2-1 (paperback edition)
978-0-9777539-2-5

ISBN 0-9777539-3-X (hardcover edition)
978-0-9777539-3-2

Distributed by Publishers Group West
(800) 788-3123 · www.pgw.com

MIX
Paper from
responsible sources
FSC® C012700
FSC
www.fsc.org

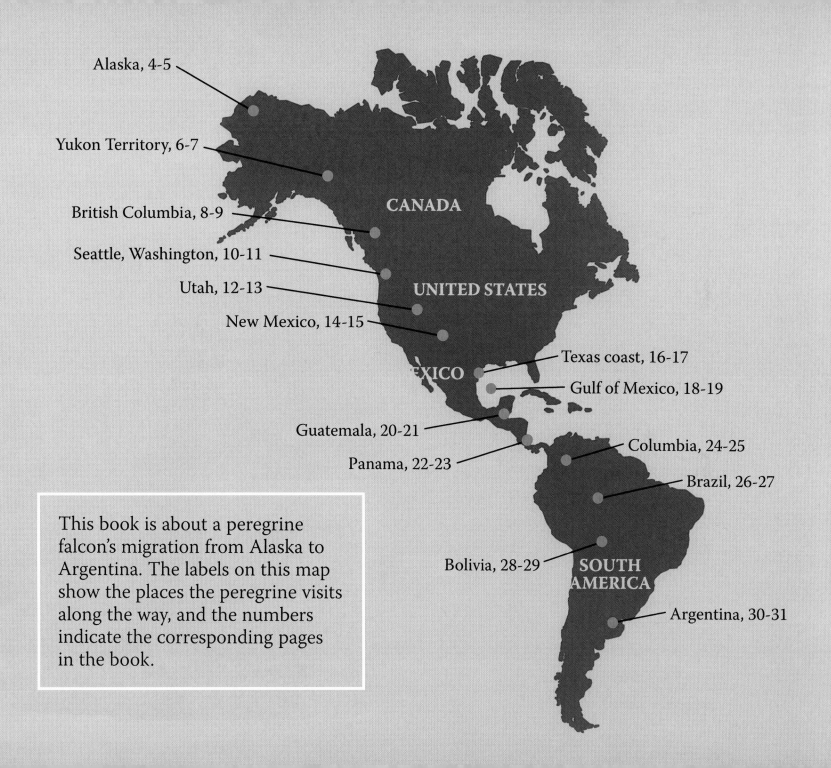

Alaska, 4-5

Yukon Territory, 6-7

British Columbia, 8-9

Seattle, Washington, 10-11

Utah, 12-13

New Mexico, 14-15

CANADA

UNITED STATES

MEXICO

Texas coast, 16-17

Gulf of Mexico, 18-19

Guatemala, 20-21

Panama, 22-23

Columbia, 24-25

Brazil, 26-27

Bolivia, 28-29

SOUTH AMERICA

Argentina, 30-31

This book is about a peregrine falcon's migration from Alaska to Argentina. The labels on this map show the places the peregrine visits along the way, and the numbers indicate the corresponding pages in the book.

The peregrine falcon wakes up on a cliff in Alaska. She perches near the nest where she raised her chicks this summer. Even though it is only September, it has already snowed and the puddles are covered with ice. She ruffles her feathers to try to keep warm, but she is restless. As each day passes, the weather will only get colder and there will be less and less sunlight. Finally, the time has come for her to leave. She takes one last look at her Alaska home, and then begins her migration south. She will fly all the way from Alaska to Argentina—a distance of more than 8,000 miles. It will take her about two months. If you tried walking that far, it would take you more than three years!

6

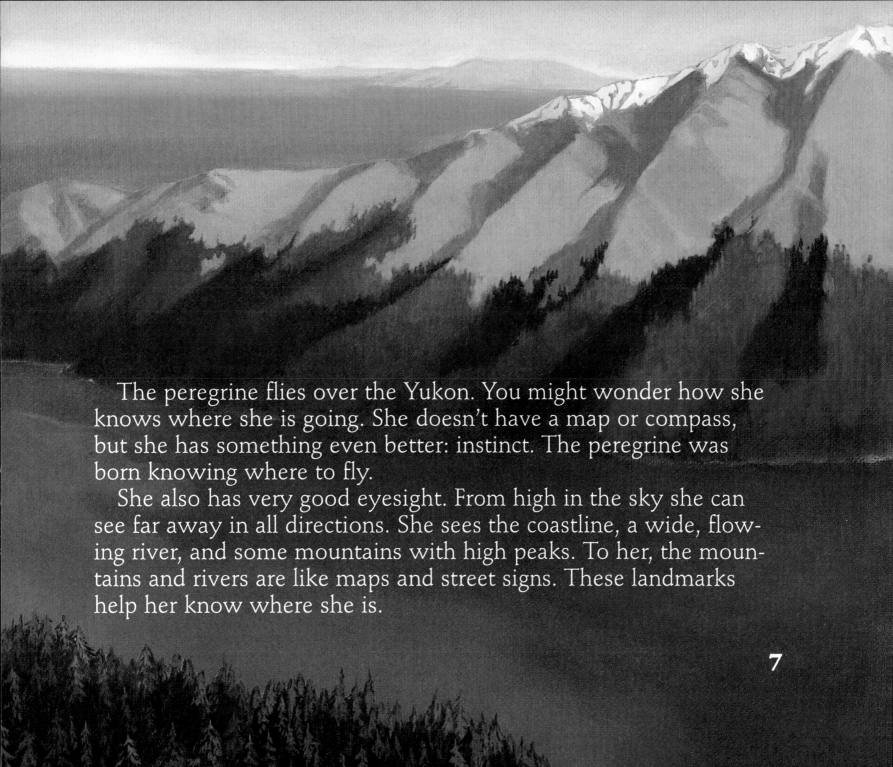

The peregrine flies over the Yukon. You might wonder how she knows where she is going. She doesn't have a map or compass, but she has something even better: instinct. The peregrine was born knowing where to fly.

She also has very good eyesight. From high in the sky she can see far away in all directions. She sees the coastline, a wide, flowing river, and some mountains with high peaks. To her, the mountains and rivers are like maps and street signs. These landmarks help her know where she is.

The peregrine arrives in British Columbia. The trees are so thick and grow so closely together that she cannot see the ground. Her wings beat up and down in a steady rhythm. She has already flown a hundred miles today. Through an opening in the trees, she sees a freeway. The peregrine is such a strong flier that she travels almost as

10

The peregrine lands in Seattle, Washington. She perches on the windowsill of an office building and looks down. Far below, amidst the honking cars, traffic lights, and rushing people, she notices something that interests her. It is a pigeon. She watches it fly from the sidewalk to a tree, and then to a building across the street. Pigeons are one of her favorite foods, so there is plenty for her to eat in the city.

The peregrine must hunt every day to feed herself. From a mountain ledge in Utah, she sees a dove flying below. She plunges off the mountain, folds her wings, and dives headfirst onto her prey. The injured dove tumbles toward Earth, but before it can hit the ground, the peregrine swoops down and catches it! She carries the dove back up to a mountain ledge, where she picks it apart with her razor-sharp beak and talons.

12

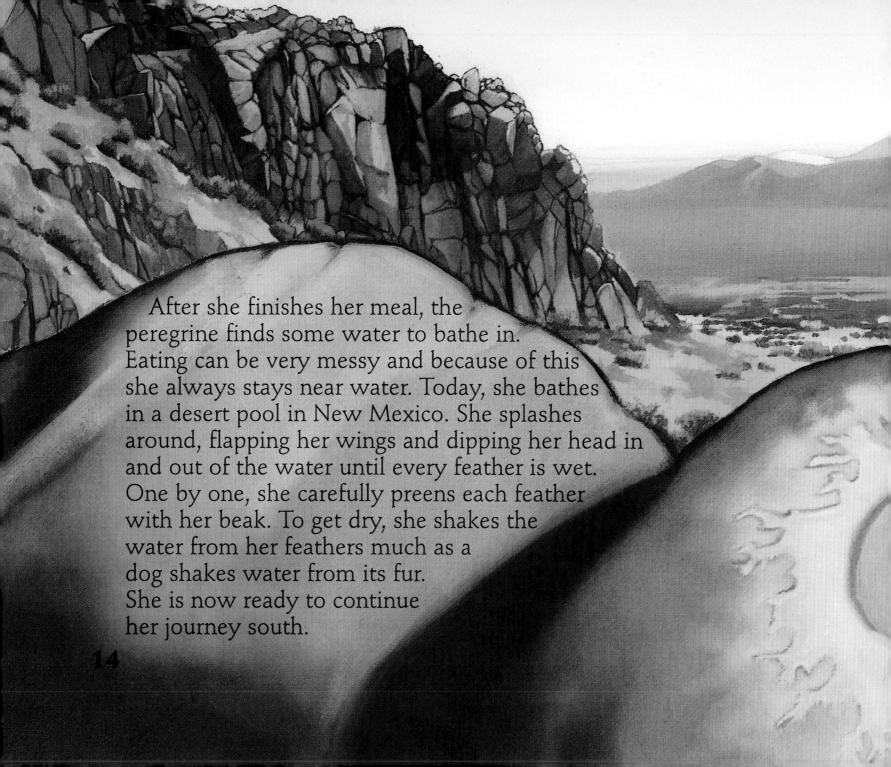

After she finishes her meal, the peregrine finds some water to bathe in. Eating can be very messy and because of this she always stays near water. Today, she bathes in a desert pool in New Mexico. She splashes around, flapping her wings and dipping her head in and out of the water until every feather is wet. One by one, she carefully preens each feather with her beak. To get dry, she shakes the water from her feathers much as a dog shakes water from its fur. She is now ready to continue her journey south.

14

15

16

She lands on the Texas coast. Many other migrating peregrines also stop here during the month of October because there are so many kinds of birds to eat. The golden plover, laughing gull, and green-winged teal are just some of the birds the peregrine hunts. She spends several days here eating and resting. At times she even plays with other peregrines. In a high-speed dance, they swoop, glide, and chase each other across the sky.

The peregrine flies over the sea, with no land in sight. From Texas she could continue to fly over land, but instead she takes a shortcut and flies over the Gulf of Mexico. At times she flies so close to the water that her wings nearly touch the waves. Several hours pass and the sun starts to set. The peregrine could fly through the night but lands on a passing ship going in her direction. She perches on the ship's mast and gently closes her eyes. The captain watches her through the night as he steers the ship through dark seas.

19

After a few days, the peregrine reaches land and is flying over Guatemala. She feels the winds pick up. Strong winds can be good or bad for the peregrine. If they are going in the wrong direction, they may blow her off course. But if they are going in the right direction, they can help her fly with a lot less effort.

Today, the winds are blowing south and she glides on them for hours, hardly flapping her wings. The winds carry her up so high that a pilot flying by can see her from his cockpit window.

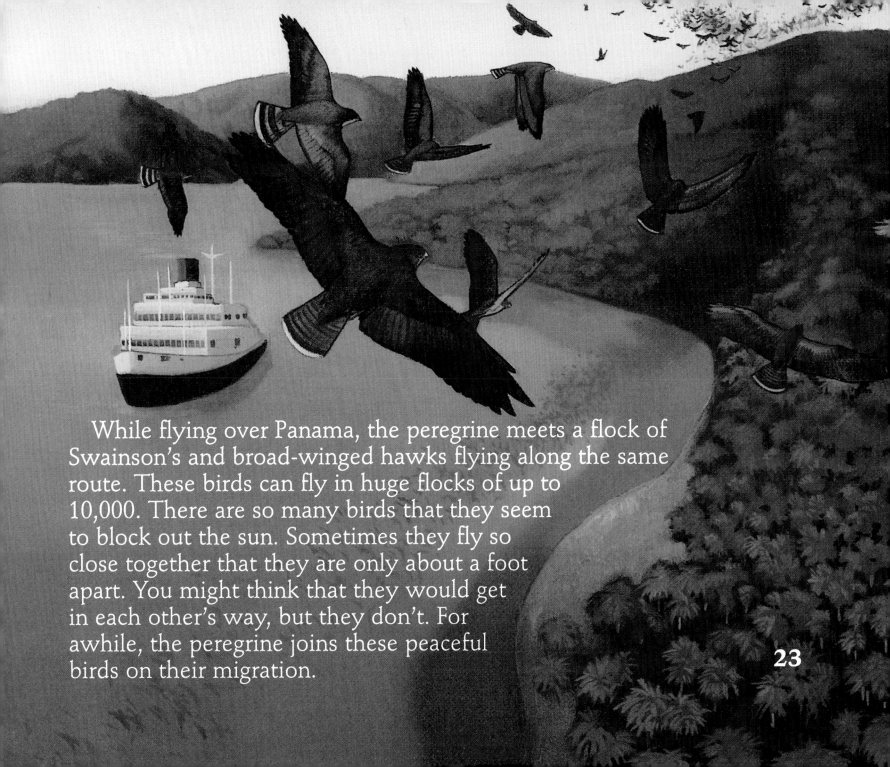

While flying over Panama, the peregrine meets a flock of Swainson's and broad-winged hawks flying along the same route. These birds can fly in huge flocks of up to 10,000. There are so many birds that they seem to block out the sun. Sometimes they fly so close together that they are only about a foot apart. You might think that they would get in each other's way, but they don't. For awhile, the peregrine joins these peaceful birds on their migration.

23

24

The peregrine flies over a forest that looks like an enormous green ocean. She is above the rain forests of Colombia. She feels thirsty and looks for some water to drink. There is plenty of water here because it rains nearly every day. The peregrine lands next to a waterfall. She dips her head in and out of the water, taking long, deep drinks. After shaking her feathers dry, the peregrine flies straight up until she is again soaring over the lush, green trees of the rain forest.

She continues flying south until she is above the rain forests of Brazil. The sky turns gray, thunder strikes, and raindrops start to fall. It is hard for her to see through the clouds and fog, and the pounding rains make her wings feel tired. She lands in a tall tree. The tree's leaves shelter her from the falling rain. The peregrine closes her eyes and takes a nap until the late afternoon. She no longer needs to fly as far each day because she is nearing the end of her journey.

Sunset comes and the peregrine lands for the night in the woodlands of Bolivia. While she is asleep, a great horned owl silently flies by, beating its powerful wings. The peregrine does not have many predators, but one creature she must be wary of is the great horned owl. This fierce-looking bird hunts her at night while she is sleeping. The owl has excellent eyesight and hearing and can usually find its prey no matter how well it is hidden. But tonight the peregrine is lucky! The owl does not notice that she is carefully nestled between two tree branches.

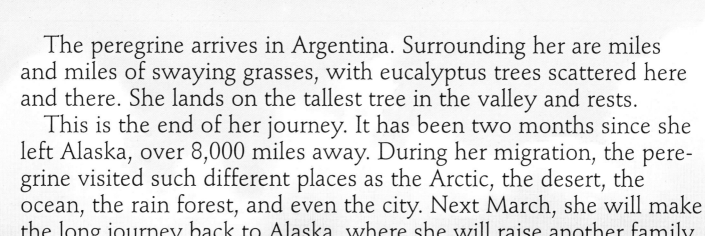

The peregrine arrives in Argentina. Surrounding her are miles and miles of swaying grasses, with eucalyptus trees scattered here and there. She lands on the tallest tree in the valley and rests.

This is the end of her journey. It has been two months since she left Alaska, over 8,000 miles away. During her migration, the peregrine visited such different places as the Arctic, the desert, the ocean, the rain forest, and even the city. Next March, she will make the long journey back to Alaska, where she will raise another family.

But for now, she is home.

THE PEREGRINE'S JOURNEY is based on the migration of a real peregrine falcon that was tracked by satellite telemetry by the U.S. Fish & Wildlife Service. The name "peregrine" means wanderer, and the peregrine falcon has one of the longest migrations of any North American bird.

The bird in this book is a tundra peregrine. Tundra-nesting falcons winter in South America, and may fly up to 18,000 miles in a year. The tundra peregrine is one of more than a dozen subspecies of peregrine falcon. Most peregrine falcons don't migrate.

Peregrine falcons live on all continents except Antarctica, and on many oceanic islands. They live in a wide variety of habitats from the tropics to the desert, from the ocean to the tundra, and from sea level to up to 12,000 feet. Peregrine falcons are raptors—which means they hunt and kill their food. Their strong, sharp, curved beaks, keen eyes for viewing prey from great distances, and sharp powerful claws (called talons) all make peregrines very well adapted for hunting.

The peregrine falcon is the fastest animal in the world in its hunting dive, the stoop, in which it soars to a great height, and then dives steeply at speeds up to 240 miles per hour onto its prey. The peregrines' incredible speed is the primary weapon used to kill their prey. When they get ready to strike, they close their talons and strike the bird in a plunging dive, either knocking the bird unconscious or killing it with a single blow. In level flight, the normal speed for peregrines is about 40-55 miles per hour.

Peregrine falcons feed almost exclusively on birds, including doves, waterfowl and songbirds. Peregrine falcons rarely suffer predation by other animals.

Great-horned owls and golden eagles are known to occasionally kill peregrines. Peregrine eggs sometimes fall victim to raccoons and foxes.

Human behavior is the greatest threat to the peregrine falcon. In the 1970s, the peregrine nearly became extinct because of the use of DDT and other pesticides, which got into the bird's food. DDT caused peregrines to lay eggs with shells so thin that they would crack before the chicks could be born. By 1975, there were estimated to be only 39 nesting pairs of peregrines in the lower 48 states, and the bird was extinct east of the Mississippi River. The peregrine falcon was declared an endangered species, and a captive breeding and release program was established to ensure the bird's survival.

Today, the peregrine falcon is doing much better. DDT is no longer used in the United States, and peregrines are now able to successfully raise their young. As a result, the peregrine falcon was removed from the endangered species list in 1999.

TO FIND OUT MORE, CONTACT:

The Peregrine Fund
www.peregrinefund.org

Santa Cruz Predatory Bird Research Group
www.scpbrg.org

Falcon Research Group
www.frg.org

HawkWatch International
www.hawkwatch.org